TUDOR
HOUSES
EXPLAINED

TREVOR YORKE

COUNTRYSIDE BOOKS
NEWBURY BERKSHIRE

First published 2009
© Trevor Yorke 2009

COUNTRYSIDE BOOKS
3 Catherine Road
Newbury, Berkshire

To view our complete range of books,
please visit us at
wwwcountrysidebooks.co.uk

ISBN 1 84674 150 0

Designed by Peter Davies, Nautilus Design
Produced through MRM Associates Ltd., Reading
Printed by Information Press, Oxford

CONTENTS

Introduction

The commanding bulk of Henry VIII in his full regalia and Queen Elizabeth I with her fiery red hair and pasty white face are mighty figures that still retain our fascination over 400 years on. The Tudor period they reigned in began with the accession of Henry's father in 1485 and lasted until the death of the queen in 1603, the latter half of which is commonly referred to as the Elizabethan Age. If the 16th century is dominated in people's minds by these iconic characters, then they can be reminded of them by the houses that still stand in our towns and villages up to 500 years later. Black and white timber framed buildings jettying out between later bland structures and rambling rows of quaint cottages around a green are as much a distinctive image of England as the monarchs themselves.

The range of houses built, however, is more diverse than would at first appear and the changes that occurred in the Tudor period more groundbreaking. At the beginning some were little different from their medieval predecessors while at the end there were notable examples that gave a taste of the century to come. Our familiar image of Tudor houses is also rather twisted by later changes made to them; many of those that still stand today appeared radically different inside and out when first built. This book sets out to explain these great changes in domestic architecture, with pictures, photos and diagrams highlighting the features and styles to help you recognise houses from this period. It also gives structural and layout clues that can help you strip away all those later changes and identify the real Tudor house beneath.

The book is divided into six chapters, covering firstly the general changes in society and how they affected the housing in the period. The second chapter explains how the structure of the house took shape, the materials used and the type of features that would have been fitted. We next look at the styles of timber framed, brick and stone houses and the details that help us date them. The fourth chapter goes inside to describe the interior and some of the features from this period that can still be found, while the fifth explains how the area around the larger Tudor house may have appeared at the time. The final chapter discusses Tudor houses after 1603 – and what aspects of them you are likely to see today.

The *Explained* series of books focuses upon structures that have survived. Tudor houses that are still standing tend, as you will discover, to be those built for the wealthier customers of the period, the homes of the mass of peasants having long since gone. As a result, this book will often refer to the largest houses as points of reference, in order to describe details on lesser buildings; they are covered in greater depth in *The Country House Explained*. Here we concentrate on what remains of old manor houses, jettied town houses, farmhouses and cottages.

Trevor Yorke

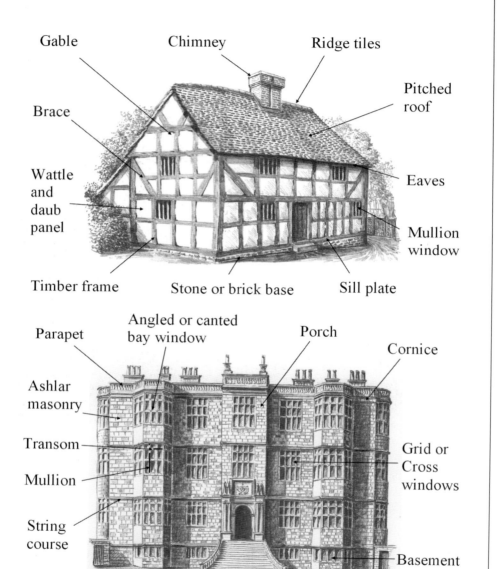

Gable

Chimney

Ridge tiles

Brace

Pitched roof

Wattle and daub panel

Eaves

Mullion window

Timber frame

Stone or brick base

Sill plate

Parapet

Angled or canted bay window

Porch

Cornice

Ashlar masonry

Transom

Mullion

Grid or Cross windows

String course

Basement

Bays

Facade

CHAPTER 1

Tudor Housing

Town and Village

FIG 1.1: THE SHAMBLES, YORK: *This offers a rare impression of how many Tudor towns would have appeared, with narrow streets and overhanging buildings jostling for space. The Shambles contains houses from the 15th century onwards, with their lower storey used as shops – in this case they were originally butchers.*

Rarely has there been a time like the 16th century when one family so dominated events, their struggles to establish a dynasty changing the course of British history. Henry Tudor, his son and grandchildren took their largely faithful population on an economic and religious roller-coaster ride, destroying medieval establishments and customs but laying the seeds for the modern state. Power began to shift from the local gentry to a rapidly expanding court and its ministers, and they expressed their control in lavish and extravagant houses. Marriage guidance counsellors were also kept busy!

When the first Tudor king, Henry

FIG 1.2: HAMPTON COURT, SURREY: *Cardinal Thomas Wolsey was Henry VIII's ambitious Chancellor and Archbishop of York although it took him 15 years before he actually visited his minster! He had spent much of his efforts building himself a palace more glorious than any house of the monarch, probably a mistake as his failure to secure a divorce for the king brought him down and this vast brick palace fell into Crown hands. It is notable as one of the first buildings to express elements of the Renaissance before the separation from the Catholic Church left us isolated from the main flow of European architectural fashions.*

VII (1485–1509) took the throne after defeating Richard III at Bosworth Field in 1485 he used marriage rather than war to secure his family's hold on power and heal over wounds, a policy that helped leave a significant surplus in the treasury on his death. Unfortunately his son, the over indulgent Henry VIII (1509–1547), managed to spend it all despite sizeable windfalls from the sale of property after he had dissolved the monasteries in the late 1530s. His children, the Protestant Edward VI (1547–53) and Catholic Mary I (1553–1558), fought over the direction of Henry's other legacy, the Church of England, before Elizabeth I (1558–1603) sought compromise to bring a tense peace to sectarian frictions. Aided by accomplished ministers, the economy recovered and the country basked in unprecedented national self-confidence, a glorious period that overshadowed her rather sour later years.

SOCIETY
Population and class

The Tudor period witnessed a reverse in the long period of population decline. Ever since it reached a peak in around 1300, poor harvests and then the Black Death had devastated all levels of society so that when Henry VII took the throne there were fewer than three million people in the country. The number grew progressively through the 16th century to around four million by 1600. At the top were the nobility, a relatively small group of powerful families, and below them an expanding class of gentlemen, including rich merchants, courtiers and men of law. Next down the ladder were the yeoman farmers, who were sometimes as rich as those above them but more interested in acquiring land than expressing their fortune in heraldic display.

Below these were the vast majority of the population, a complicated and regionalised range of people from tenant farmers down to landless labourers. More than half of these lived on or below the subsistence level, only able to supply themselves with sufficient food, clothing and shelter to survive. The situation for the poor worsened through much of the 16th century as wages could not keep up with inflation, enclosures in some parts of the country deprived them of land, and the Dissolution of the Monasteries took away a vital source of charity. Poverty grew and vagrancy was a constant source of problems for polite society, especially in London.

One of the after effects of the Black Death was the breakdown of the rigid feudal system, with landowners finding it difficult to keep labourers tied to one location when there were too few people to do the work. Although this situation varied from area to area it gave some lower down the social ladder the opportunity to escape poverty and acquire land. By the 16th century there were families whose growing wealth enabled their sons to gain an education and, as a result, a position at court or in law, and the classification of 'gentry'.

Wealth and trade

The majority of the population were involved in agriculture and although many lost out in villages where there was a restructuring of the land, the larger, more securely tenanted farmer could prosper, especially as food prices increased steadily through the century. Many of these changes came about due to the high price of wool, which more than tripled in price by mid century, and landowners converted arable areas to pasture, which required less labour, only for some to convert it back later when the price fell!

FIG 1.3: NEWSTEAD ABBEY, NOTTINGHAMSHIRE:
The break with Rome initiated by Henry VIII's demand for a divorce from his first wife gave the Crown the opportunity to dissolve the monasteries and acquire their land and wealth. The religious houses were in part initiators of their own downfall as many orders had abused their position in the public's eyes and Henry exploited their unpopularity. He first had the smaller establishments closed in 1535–6 and then the larger abbeys in 1538–40. The priory in this picture had the cloisters converted into a country house, while the church was stripped of its assets and just the shell remains today.

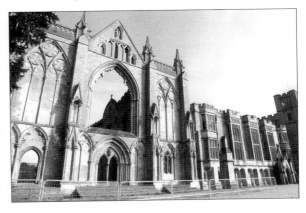

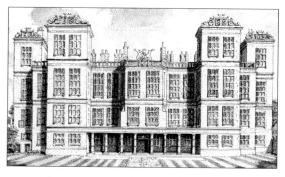

FIG 1.4: HARDWICK HALL, DERBYSHIRE: *There was now greater fluidity in society than there had been in the medieval period, though for women riches could only be gained through marriage. One of the most notorious 16th-century ladies was Elizabeth of Shrewsbury, whose family were bankrupt squires two generations before; through calculated marriages she amassed a fortune and became the richest woman in England after the queen. Her final glory was Hardwick Hall, designed by Robert Smythson, the leading mason of the time, and built overlooking her earlier project, the Old Hall, which was barely finished before she started this one! Its mass of glass was characteristic of the spectacular country houses built in the last decades of the 16th century, the towers at each corner acting partly as buttresses to support the walls weakened by all the windows.*

Industry began to prosper under the Tudors. Textiles were the most profitable but mining, quarrying, smelting iron and shipbuilding became important in certain areas, increasing the consumption of wood and charcoal, which began to deprive the house builder of the best timber and the householder of fuel for fires. In response coal, which had been limited to areas where it was freely available, was in growing demand in the major towns and cities that could be reached by coastal vessels, principally coming from the Newcastle area (this was known as sea coal).

Town and country

Most people lived in villages and hamlets. These were not the neat and trim chocolate box image that we might imagine today but a working community with poor roads and a scattered appearance, albeit surrounded by well managed fields and woodland. The more established farmers had enough land to provide much of what they needed; however, those with small plots or no land were vulnerable when times were hard. No one was completely self sufficient, all relying to some degree on the markets, fairs and local towns where they could buy goods.

With the exception of London, which had a population of around a quarter of a million by 1600, most urban areas were small by today's standards. Bristol, Norwich and York had between 10,000 and 20,000 residents but all the other towns had less – some were barely more than a large village. While many grew relatively rapidly in this period, especially ports and centres connected with successful trades like wool, a few fared less well with business lost after the end of pilgrimages, the Dissolution of the Monasteries and the silting up of rivers. Where there was expansion, little of it was planned; roads were usually unpaved, drains rare and running water available to only an exceptional few. As a result, outbreaks of disease

and fire were severe, both spreading rapidly through the congested timber framed communities.

HOUSING

The general improvement in the standard of living and increased wealth of those in a fortunate position was reflected by a rise in the number of houses erected in the Tudor period. This was especially notable in the second half of the century, with the stability of the Elizabethan Age encouraging many to spend their income on the latest timber framed,

FIG 1.5: *The Reformation of the 1530s and the more intense actions taken in Edward's reign resulted in the removal of images and ended pilgrimages to holy sites, depriving a number of towns and cities of the trade which they had formerly relied upon from pilgrims. It also made those who wished to hear Catholic mass from then on worship in secret and hide their allegiance through ingenious plans of houses and decorative symbols. Travelling priests had to be hidden out of view of the authorities when they came knocking, so priest holes in which they could hide were built by Catholic families. In this example, it was under the altar in the middle of the picture. The priests may have been less appreciative though if they had known it used to be a garderobe (toilet)!*

FIG 1.6: NANTWICH, CHESHIRE: *Most towns suffered some degree of devastation from fire during this period, a problem intensified by the lack of planning and tightly packed timber framed houses. Nantwich had such a fate in 1583 and many of its timber framed buildings in the town centre date from the rebuilding afterwards, including the impressive Crown Hotel built in 1585 with a fashionable mass of windows.*

FIG 1.7: LAVENHAM, SUFFOLK:
Although a village in size today, this was an important town in the 15th and 16th centuries and is still blessed with timber framed houses built with wealth from the wool trade.

structure. They were generally individual properties built for or by the householder for their own use; there was little speculative building and planned developments or rows of cottages were rare. In some towns regulations put a thin stone wall between properties to reduce the risk of fire spreading, while others preferred a gap between properties to avoid boundary disputes. Architects were unknown in this period, instead local masons and carpenters of varying skill would often plan and build houses, with the builder (landowner) having the responsibility for supplying materials and sometimes labour.

Large houses

The grand houses of the nobility and gentry were still designed with defence in mind in the early Tudor period, even if this was rather more for display than actual conflict. A common arrangement was to have a battlemented wall surrounding a courtyard, with the scattered components of the house looking in upon each other and with the principal building, the hall, sited at the opposite end from the entrance gatehouse.

In the second half of the period this began to change. The Dissolution of the Monasteries released a huge number of estates and properties into the Crown's hands and many were sold to the nobility and gentry and some to the new up and coming rich. They would often asset strip their new acquisitions, sell off building material, restructure the farmland and increase rents, but most did not rebuild the main house until the more religiously settled times of Elizabeth's reign.

By then the style of country house was changing. As a larger proportion

stone or brick structure, displaying their success and ambitions in its decoration. This Great Rebuilding (a term coined by the 20th century historian W.G. Hoskins) affected areas at different times. It was already underway in counties like Sussex and Kent when Henry VII took the throne; in the south, east and the Midlands it peaked in the late 16th and early 17th century, while highland areas to the north and west were in some cases as late as the 18th and 19th centuries.

Most new houses were built on the site of older ones, and sometimes even included parts of its former

FIG 1.8: *A manor house in 1485 (right) and then again in 1603 (top). Many houses like this may not have had a total rebuild in this period but would have additions and alterations to change their appearance. In the 1485 image (right) the house is set within its walls, with the main hall across the middle facing the entrance to the fortified courtyard. In the later view of the same house (top), it has new private chambers and guestrooms added to a more up-to-date hall, which has gained a porch and large bay window. The gatehouse has been rebuilt into an imposing structure with additional accommodation for important visitors, while a large garden has been created at the rear by extending the old walls. For all the change the manor house still stands on the same site within the village; in most communities it would not be until the late 17th century and after that more dramatic rebuilding and re-siting of large houses would take place.*

of the gentry became courtiers and tied to the monarch they were less likely to rebel and hence there was little need for a defensive house. Late 16th-century structures looked outwards, with generally symmetrical façades and masses of glass windows. The largest houses were often built with a visit from Queen Elizabeth in mind, as she rather shrewdly spent little on her own palaces, preferring her subjects to fight amongst themselves to accommodate her huge household train in ever more elaborate and lavish structures, referred to as 'prodigy houses'. These, however, along with the more modest homes of the lesser gentry, tended to be built close to the building they replaced or on the same site. Where these houses today are surrounded by countryside it is often because the village they were originally next to was re-sited at a later date to create a landscape park.

Urban properties

In towns and cities the expanding urban population was generally squeezed into the existing town boundary on previously open sites, old monastic properties or by encroaching on market places and castle grounds. Urban house plots tended to be long and thin with the narrow, pointed gable end facing onto the street and the outbuildings and garden stretching out behind. Although sometimes two or more of these plots were combined to allow for a larger house, most owners were restricted to a 15 ft to 25 ft wide frontage; as a result, many expanded upwards with extra floors jettied out, making already narrow streets even more congested.

Rural housing

Villages varied greatly in their administration and physical appearance, not just due to the type of farming in a particular region but also to how tightly the lord of the manor controlled it. Some communities already had their great medieval open fields enclosed into individual farm holdings while others developed in a more scattered manner with little attention from the landowner. Others slowly petered out and died as the dwindling population

was moved out and more profitable sheep were brought in to graze on the previously arable fields.

Those local landowners who benefited from the changes and a rising price of produce at market built themselves new houses of two or three storeys. The manor house was usually still within the village at this date, although in many areas its role as the business centre of a feudal community had changed as new tenants required less contact with the more private home of the lord.

Farmers with large holdings could expect a house with two principal ground floor rooms and chambers above. Others with smaller holdings or a trade would usually have more humble accommodation, a single

---

FIG 1.9: *In this period houses and shops often begin to encroach upon medieval market places, as in this example where the original long, wide space has been cut down in size by an island of houses and shops. This encroachment became more widespread in the following centuries.*

FIG 1.10: *A timber framed farmhouse based on an example at the Weald and Downland Museum in Sussex. It has two ground floor rooms heated by back-to-back fireplaces in the middle, with unheated bedchambers above. Although only modest accommodation by today's standards, this was a big step forward for the average Tudor yeoman farmer.*

storey cottage or longhouse with a main room for the family, and in some cases a separate byre for livestock under the same roof. Below this would be the simplest and poorest housing, which lacked the quality materials and professional construction of the farmers' houses; the labourers' cottages in most areas were only expected to last a few generations and all are long since gone.

With this in mind, it is worth remembering that the Tudor houses you see around you today, and which are featured in this book, were the best of their day and built for the wealthier members of the community. A quaint timber framed cottage with a couple of low beamed rooms on each floor should rightly impress us with its quality of build as it has stood for so long, but the owner of the same social standing today would expect a larger detached house with numerous bedrooms and all mod cons. Direct comparisons such as this are never that simple but what these Tudor houses do represent is the first step to a more even distribution of the nation's wealth. They are tangible evidence that even those from a poor background could now – through education, ambition and hard work – improve their standing in society and they chose to display it with fine new houses.

CHAPTER 2

Tudor Houses

MATERIALS AND STRUCTURE

FIG 2.1: LITTLE MORETON HALL, CHESHIRE: *This Tudor courtyard house built over successive generations by the Moreton family illustrates that even the houses of the wealthy were still being constructed from local materials in styles popular with the region in which they were located. The south range in this picture, dating from the second half of the 16th century, has the latest fashionable feature of an immense long gallery perched on top yet it is still medieval in appearance with no attempt to introduce Renaissance symmetry or classical detailing.*

The houses built in the late 15th and throughout the 16th century are examples of vernacular architecture as, with the exception of some of the grandest buildings, they were constructed with local materials by local craftsmen. This was mainly due to the limitations of transport, which meant that materials like timber and stone were very expensive to carry even a short distance. Masons and carpenters also rarely worked outside their local area and hence the methods they used were passed down from generation to generation, with little outside influence. This created regional forms and styles of house, with colours that tied them into the surrounding landscape. It was only the wealthy who could afford to employ a renowned mason or, if they lived close to navigable rivers and the coast, were able to get different materials shipped to buck this trend.

The builder in the case of most Tudor houses was the landowner or householder and he was responsible for providing materials, transport and labour. The mason, brick-maker or carpenter generally only brought with them their personal tools and skill. When a large brick or stone structure was involved, the Tudor building site must have been a noisy, sprawling enterprise with stones being cut to size or bricks fired in temporary kilns around the construction of the house itself. Timber framed houses were prefabricated in a yard or on site with carpenters' marks numbering joints so that they could be correctly reassembled as the house was being erected.

Despite external appearances, houses large and small were still restricted by heavy roofing materials, which required a steep pitch to take their weight, making spanning wide spaces difficult. As a result, most Tudor houses are only one room deep;

FIG 2.2: *For the poorer members of the community building a house was probably more of a family effort. Low walls of rough stones, layers of dried mud and straw (cob) or a flimsy timber frame supported a thatched roof, with smoke from an open fire percolating through the ridge. These one or two room, single storey cottages varied in quality and features across the regions but in the worst cases may have required rebuilding every twenty to thirty years.*

they were, however, arranged in a courtyard or with projecting wings – so appeared to be something much deeper. This suited the still largely medieval internal layout of most modest houses, which were based around a hall with rooms directly adjoining each other. However, in larger houses, especially later in the period as they sought to imitate the latest arrangements at court, difficulties arose in combining this with the classical demands of symmetry and it would not be until the 17th century that a pleasing balance between the structure, façade and internal layout of country houses would be achieved.

BRICK

The Tudor period was the first great age of brickwork. This was a high status material and those who could afford it flaunted their wealth, especially in the first half of the 16th century, with decorative patterns in walls, elaborate mouldings around doors and twisting or fluted chimneys. If they could not stretch to the complete house being made from brick it could be used as an infill in a timber frame – or if not that, then a chimney stack might be within the budget!

Romans first introduced bricks to England but the techniques for making them were lost after their departure and it was not until the 13th century that brick-makers from the Low Countries imported their skills into the east of the country. With only patchy outcrops of good building stone in this area, brick provided a distinctive and more fire-proof alternative to timber framed structures for the wealthy. In the 16th century, brick was still mainly limited to the eastern and southern counties, only later in the period spreading into the Midlands, but remaining rare in the north and west of the country.

Bricks were generally made on site in the Tudor period; there were few permanent brickworks, except in London where there was a more reliable demand. The brick-maker would have to first establish where there was suitable clay on the site or in the locality, and then when sufficient was extracted the clumps were spread over a flat area and left through the winter to be broken down by the frost. In spring the clay was watered and trodden underfoot whilst any stones were removed, before it was cut to shape, using moulds, stacked and left to dry for a few months. At an arranged time during the summer the bricks would be re-stacked to form a kiln and fired, this crude but effective method creating different finishes, depending on their position with relation to the heat.

Bricks were of irregular size in this period but generally their outward faces (stretchers) were 9–10 inches long and their short ends (headers) 4–5 inches wide. More notably, Tudor bricks were thinner than modern types, usually around 2–2¼ inches, and this was emphasised by the thicker layers of mortar used between them – even as deep as an inch in some cases. Brick walls for houses had considerable depth in the 16th century; they tended to be 1½ bricks or 13–15 inches thick, and the way they were arranged (bonding) varied, with no clear, uniform pattern in many situations. Where one is found, then

FIG 2.3: MAPLEDURHAM HOUSE, OXFORDSHIRE: *A large Elizabethan manor house built in brick for Sir Richard Blount in the last decades of the 16th century (some features were added in the late Georgian period).*

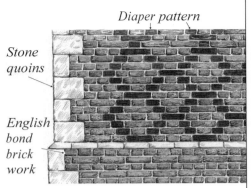

FIG 2.5: *An example of Tudor brickwork with labels of some of its distinctive features.*

FIG 2.4: *Tudor bricks were more irregular than later types, with large mortar gaps between to allow for imperfections. This example is laid out in an English bond, having alternate courses of short headers and long stretchers.*

the English bond with alternate layers of stretchers and headers facing out was popular, or variations of it with additional bands of stretchers.

Mortar was mixed on site from lime, sand and water. The lime was made by burning chalk or limestone and then combining it with water; this was beaten before sand was laid over it, and the mix was then left to stand for up to a few months. Black mortar was sometimes used, simply by adding coal dust into the mix, and a special cement made from resins and wax was used where water might penetrate a wall.

Most Tudor bricks were red, with those that had been overheated in the kiln and had turned grey used to create decorative patterns in the walls. This was a distinctive feature of Tudor houses especially in the early 16th century although it was still used in some areas well into the 17th. The most common form was a diagonal grid (diaper patterns); in some they are regularly spaced, in others more scattered within the wall. Stone was sometimes used in conjunction with brick for the corner stones (quoins), window and door surrounds and for decorative features like balustrades and plaques. In some cases this effect was replicated by plastering or painting over moulded bricks. Terracotta, a form of moulded brick made from very fine clay, was used in the same manner in a few houses in the reign of Henry VIII.

STONE

Stone has always been the first choice building material and was used in the finest houses wherever it was available in easy reach. Limestone is found in a broad band from Somerset diagonally across the country up to Yorkshire, including the Cotswolds and Northamptonshire. Sandstone

FIG 2.6: *The best stone houses were faced with fine cut stone called ashlar (left), although it was usually just for the outside, with either brick (middle) or rubble (right) used in the core of the wall.*

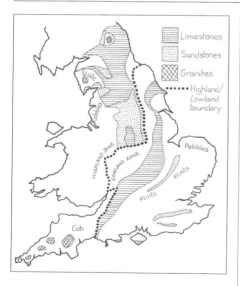

FIG 2.7: *Map of the main areas of stone building in England (it does not include smaller localised outcrops). The map is divided by the dotted line into the highland zone in the west and north and the lowland zone to the east and south.*

was used in Sussex, the West and the North Midlands and Cumbria. Both of these stones (known as freestones) are sedimentary and are easier for masons to work into shape or to form into more elaborate carvings.

Granite, however, is an igneous rock (volcanic) and very hard to cut. Where it was used in the South-West and parts of North-West England it tends to be in simple blocks. Large slabs of slate were used for walls in some parts of the west while in the east of the country flint and a hard type of chalk called clunch were sometimes used to make decorative chequer-board patterns.

Stone was expensive and limited in many areas, not just because of the poor transport system but also as there were not any large-scale quarries mass-producing masonry. There were a number of permanent sites in the finest stone areas but in most parts small local quarries that opened up perhaps for one house or a period of rebuilding were more common. In some places, stone was just extracted where it appeared in patches near to the surface leaving fields with scattered craters, which can still be sometimes found around villages today. For those lower down the social ladder who could not afford a mason, stone was used as it was found, and set in mortar or stacked dry to form rubble walls.

TIMBER FRAMING

The most widely used material for houses was timber, arranged to form frames and infilled with wattle and daub, oak laths or occasionally brick. Even in areas of good stone and established brick-making, timber framed houses were common. Oak was the first choice in most cases, with chestnut, elm and poplar also used. Shortages of timber, which would in later centuries be a major problem, were at this date limited to certain places like the locality of some shipbuilding yards and early industrial areas. Despite stories that timber from old ships was used in the frame of certain houses there is little proof for this and it is likely that one of the contemporary grades of wood which was referred to as 'ship timber' has been misinterpreted at some time (just as today you can use 'marine plywood' at home).

There are two structurally different forms of timber framed house. A crucks frame used slightly curving tree trunks cut in two down their length;

each half was placed opposite the other to create a ridge tent structure that carried the weight of the roof and from which the outer wall was projected. A box frame house is simply, as the name suggests, a framework of vertical and horizontal timbers forming the shape of the house and carrying its load through this outside wall. To prevent this wooden grid simply leaning over, diagonal braces were fitted, usually in the corners and sometimes recessed out of sight so as not to spoil the appearance of a façade. Crucks frames were becoming rare in large houses by the 16th century and were confined to locations in the highland region. It was the various styles of box frame house that were dominant and so characteristic of the Tudor period.

FIG 2.8: *A drawing of the skeleton of a box frame house, with labels of its main features.*

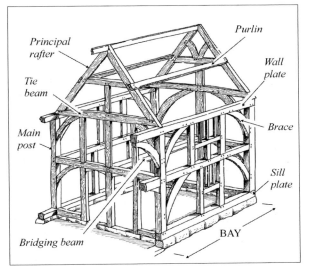

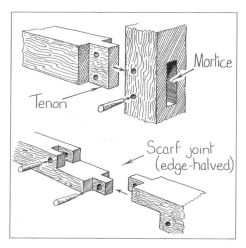

FIG 2.9: *The most common joints found in timber framed houses were the mortice and tenon (top) and the scarf joint (bottom). As the tenon is inserted in the mortice it cannot be created without dismantling the frame and hence where one is found pegged in place it is a sign of original work. The scarf was used to join two pieces together to make a longer beam and the type shown is just one of a wide variety that developed.*

Building a frame

To achieve a roughly level foundation, the lower horizontal beam, the sill plate, of a box frame house rested upon short supports during construction with the small gap above ground filled in by a low stone or brick wall afterwards. In some areas of the north the vertical beams rested directly on stone pads with the sill plate joined into their sides. The oak for the frame was usually unseasoned, and it would take years for these thick pieces to dry out completely and to stop them warping and cracking. This made

the wood easier to work with but gave houses the distinctive, slightly twisted appearance. Smaller detailed work like doorframes, windows and floors would be seasoned as their appearance and fitting was more critical, and these thinner pieces could be left outside with air gaps between them or immersed in water and dried in a kiln to speed up the process.

The timber was cut to size by hand, with large pieces sawn over an elongated pit – with one person having the unfortunate job of holding the saw below the log and getting a face full of dust. Joints were cut at this stage so the individual wall frames could be assembled on the ground and marks made to enable the prefabricated structure to be easily reassembled on site. The frames were raised into position and joined to the previous wall, slowly spreading out horizontally with each space between a cross wall called a bay (the size and arrangement of the façades of all houses are referred to in bays).

Infill

When the frame was complete the gaps in between were filled in. The most common method of infilling was wattle and daub. Thin sticks, usually hazel, were fitted vertically between the beams with horizontal pieces woven in and out of them to create a wicker panel (the wattle). Then mud, dung, straw and other local materials were mixed (the daub) and forced onto the panel inside and out to make a clay-like surface flush with the surrounding timber. In some areas oak laths were inserted into grooves in the frame rather than wattle. Brick could be used in higher class housing as an infill, characteristically arranged

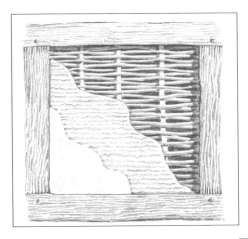

in a diagonal herringbone pattern. It is likely, however, that much of what you see today was fitted in more recent centuries, replacing original wattle and daub – more regular, machine-made bricks will indicate this. Brick does not make a good infilling, it is a lot heavier than wattle and daub and can affect a frame that was originally designed for a lighter material; it also absorbs damp and heat, creating problems with rot and poor heat retention.

The external surface of the timber framed house could be finished in a number of ways. In parts of the

FIG 2.10: *A panel of wattle and daub showing the layers of daub built up upon the wickerwork wattle.*

FIG 2.11: *Four types of box framing on higher class houses. Medieval work tends to have larger rectangular spaces between thicker and more irregular pieces of timber, usually with prominent arched braces. In general, later Tudor timber frames used more regular and fewer substantial pieces of wood in their construction. Square framing with gaps of around 2 ft to 3 ft was popular in Tudor houses from the south coast up into Cheshire. Kentish framing with a large brace running from the side down onto the sill plate was often a feature of medieval houses, especially in the South-East although it was found on many urban properties in the 16th century. Close studding originated in the eastern counties but by the Tudor period was being used across the south of the country and into the Midlands and North-East by many to display their wealth (see also figs 3.18– 3.20).*

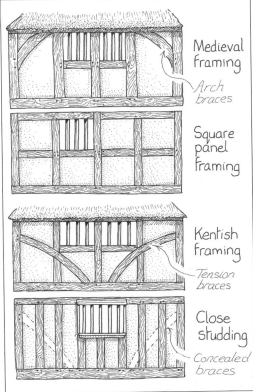

Medieval framing
Arch braces

Square panel framing

Kentish framing
Tension braces

Close studding
Concealed braces

east, weatherboarding was used, with over-lapping horizontal oak and elm boards pegged to the outside surface (most weatherboarded houses standing today are later, with cheaper wood nailed over the frame). From the second half of the 16th century pargeting was popular in some eastern counties; layers of plaster coating the frame and infill were built up to form raised patterns.

In finer timber framed houses, though, the structure formed part of the decorative scheme, with the intermediate pieces either in a tightly packed vertical arrangement called close studding (see fig 3.18) or in squares around 2 ft across known as square panelling (see fig 3.19).

FIG 2.12: *A section of exposed cob walling showing some of the components in its construction before being coated in a protective rendering (right-hand side).*

The latter could have further timber pieces inserted to form patterns called decorative framing (see fig 3.20).

How the outer surface of the house was finished is still a matter of debate and there were certainly regional if not personal variations. Many would have left the oak unfinished so it naturally turned silvery grey with the wattle and daub infills between being painted or simply limewashed. In some cases this limewash may have been applied over the timber structure as well. It is likely that most streets full of better class timber framed houses were colourful, with panels in tones of yellows, reds and pinks highlighting the patterns of timber, and with different colours favoured in certain regions. Blackened timber with white panels was probably only used in a few locations, such as Cheshire; the stark black and white scheme we are familiar with today was a Victorian creation and the modern appearance of many of our Tudor timber framed houses is not as originally intended.

Cob

A widely used building material, especially in the South West, was cob. The distinctive broad, tapering walls were made from layers of mud mixed with straw and other materials and built up in slabs. As long as the top and bottom were kept dry and it had a protective coating the wall could last for centuries. Forms of this were probably used in many locations for poor housing, long since gone and only recorded in raised banks in deserted villages.

Roofs

Thatch was the most common roofing material for the houses of the masses,

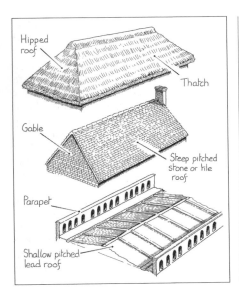

FIG 2.13: *Examples of roof types and coverings used in the Tudor period.*

FIG 2.14: *(right) Examples of roof trusses. In the south and east of the country crown post roofs were widely used in the finest houses but fell from favour early in the Tudor period, with clasped purlin roofs with similar sized rafters and the purlins held between the collar and principal rafter becoming more common. This type was also found in some highland areas during the 16th century. In areas where crucks frames had formerly been popular, such as the Midlands, new box frame houses had trenched purlin trusses with distinctive heavy principal rafters much thicker than the common rafters between each truss. In the north of England king post roof trusses were used throughout this period with a large central post and slender purlins trenched into the principal rafters.*

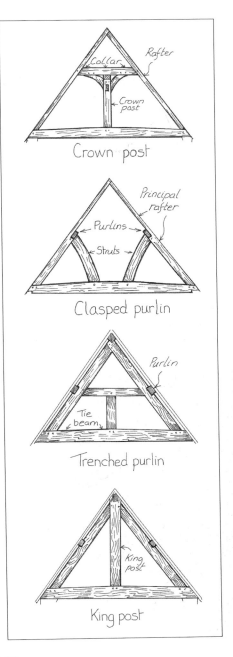

requiring a steep pitched roof of 50° to 60° – a hipped roof with the slope on all four sides or a pitched roof with a gable at each end, often raised up to protect the edge of the roofing material, with a stepped profile popular in the east of the country. Oak shingles, flat wooden tiles, may still have been used in some areas. Better class housing could have alternative coverings. Clay tiles were made in a similar way to bricks and they were widely used on steep pitched roofs in London and the east during this period and elsewhere by the late 16th century (pantiles are likely not to have been imported until the 17th century). Blue slates were shipped by sea from Devon and Cornwall and were used in parts of the South East. Flat slabs of sandstone and limestone may also have been used where the stone occurred but the methods for splitting them into thinner pieces are not recorded until the end of the period. Welsh and Cumbrian slate is likely to have been used where it was extracted but does not seem to have spread widely out of these areas.

Lead became an important roofing material as more elaborate houses required it for drainage, glazing and covering the tops of the turrets that became such a feature of Tudor housing. Its light weight also meant those who could afford it used lead to cover whole roofs, which could have a very shallow pitch and could be hidden out of sight of those below behind a classical parapet. Although lead mining expanded in this period, much of the demand was for reused sheets, a vast quantity being sold off from churches and abbeys after the Dissolution of the Monasteries.

The arrangement of timber beams that supported the roof from within –

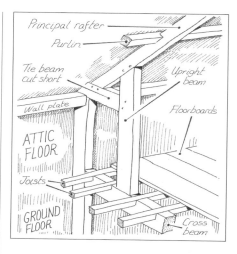

FIG 2.15: *In many later houses, especially small types, the roof area was used as an upper storey, in which case the tie beam was cut back and a vertical or diagonal post ran up across its end for support (there would be a short horizontal collar above to tie in the principal rafters).*

trusses – can be key to dating houses. Changes in style and development in carpentry are most evident here and as the space is often left untouched by later revisions a peek into the loft space can be most revealing!

Windows

The window in a timber framed house was usually part of the structure, with the vertical divisions – mullions – being fitted into the horizontal lintel and sill within an opening in the frame. A horizontal cross-beam, a transom, could also be fitted and these were popular in the large windows found in the late 16th century. In a stone or brick house a separate frame was inset into the wall. Tudor houses of this type also had a hood mould fitted above individual windows, a horizontal lip that turned down at each end and kept rain off the opening below.

Windows that projected out from the wall, either resting on the ground and covering one or more storeys (bay window) or bracketed off the wall (oriel window), were used (see fig 2.17), the latter being particularly popular on Tudor houses. Bay windows were only found on some high status properties, angled or square sided in most cases and a few rounded at the end of the period. Timber framed oriel windows usually had decorative brackets or a plain coving beneath, although some early 16th century examples rested on a large wooden sill, which was richly carved. Many timber framed houses had shallow projecting windows fitted; they did not protrude as far as an oriel (see fig 1.7) and were simply pegged to the frame (see fig 3.24).

The windows in many houses in this period still used the medieval methods of keeping out the elements – oiled cloth or wooden shutters fitted on the inside. Glass was an expensive luxury used in the houses of the nobility when Henry VII came to the throne and it was still the practice to take the window with you when you moved! By the end of the period it was becoming common further down the social ladder, in the dwellings of merchants, yeoman farmers and many

FIG 2.16: *A simple mullion window (top) with internal shutters and a large late Tudor glazed window (bottom) with labels of its parts. The hood or label mould and diamond shaped panes are distinctive features of Tudor windows.*

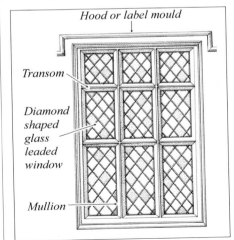

Hood or label mould

Transom

Diamond shaped glass leaded window

Mullion

Doors

As with windows, the doorway was either formed out of an opening in a timber structure or from a separate solid wooden or stone frame, with the door itself usually resting up against the inner face (only recessed in the finest houses). These surrounds were mostly rectangular in shape with a shallow arched, pointed or ogee shaped doorhead across the top. The triangular shaped panels (spandrels) on these could be plain, recessed or decorated. Large semi-circular topped doors were introduced to some late prodigy houses (see fig 3.15). The edge of the frame was often moulded or chamfered, with the profile continuing down each side (jambs), although Tudor examples often stop two-thirds of the way down and not near the bottom as in other periods.

Doors in this period were formed from vertical planks with horizontal battens to hold them together on the inside. Sometimes the whole inner face could be fitted with horizontal boards, making a flush, double thickness door. Most 16th century doors are distinguished from later versions by having only two or three wide planks of different widths with four or five battens across the back. In finer examples the outside face could have thin wooden fillet strips covering the gaps to keep draughts and rain out. These ran across the top of the long metal strap hinges, which were hung off vertical

FIG 2.17: *An oriel window (left) and a bay window (right).*

urban properties. The individual panes were made from spun glass, blown out down a tube and rotated to form a disc, which was then cut into diamond shaped pieces (quarrels) – this old glass can usually be identified by its green/yellow tinge, irregular surface and the tiny bubbles within. These were then fixed into lead cames to hold them in place, the distinctive diamond shapes of Tudor windows having the advantage that small or broken fragments could still be used for the pieces around the edge. The fragile glazed window was usually strengthened by a vertical rod called a stanchion down the middle, which was connected by wire to the lead. One of the window lights would often be hinged (casements) while others had metal vents in place of a pane, either single ones or in a line, sometimes with delicate patterns.

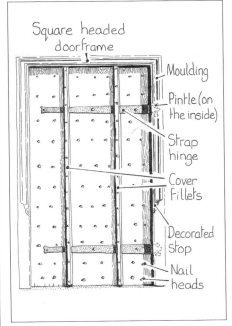

FIG 2.19: *A door and surround with labels of their parts. The square headed doorway shown was the most widely used in the 16th century, with the best examples having a moulded surround (finishing high off the ground in the mid and late 16th century). Before banks became common in the 18th century, money was kept at home so security was important. Locks, bolts and even drawbars were fitted.*

FIG 2.18: *Although doors have often been replaced, the frame or head frequently survive, sometimes with dates in the lintel above. Four-centred arches with plain or decorated spandrels (top), cambered doorheads (middle) and ogee-shaped ones (bottom) were common on important entrances.*

bracketed pins (pintles) set in the door frame or wall. Those houses influenced by the Renaissance could have more elaborate patterned doors with strips fixed to the face to make separate panels (true panelled doors did not become common until the late 17th century).

FIG 2.20: *Three examples of chimneys that can be found on Tudor houses. A stout stack fitted on the ridge of the house (left) was distinctive of lowland axial plan houses (see fig 3.5). Tall decorative chimneys (middle) were fitted along the outer wall of the finest houses; keeping the top of the chimney above the ridge was important for not disrupting the draw. On Elizabethan prodigy houses this type (right) was shaped to fit in with the classical theme of the decoration.*

Chimneys

To most Tudors an enclosed fireplace and a flue to draw off the smoke was the height of modernity and a luxury, which they displayed externally with tall, highly decorative chimneys. Originally, in medieval timber framed halls, the smoke from the central open hearth simply permeated through the roof or in large houses through louvres in the ridge. Later, some had the fire placed against a wall, either with a hood or a screen above to collect the fumes. This was still being done in some Tudor houses, although by the time of the Great Rebuilding in the second half of the 16th century the inclusion of a brick or stone chimney and fireplace was a key element in the plan.

Many chimneys of this date were simply planted on the outside wall, especially where they were fitted to an existing house. In a new building the chimney could be incorporated in an external wall with a row of tall chimneys serving a number of fireplaces. A distinctive form in this period, especially in the lowland region, was to have a stout, square block roughly in the centre of the roof ridge and in line with the front door.

CHAPTER 3

Tudor Style

PLANS AND DECORATION

FIG 3.1: WOLLATON HALL, NOTTINGHAM: *This late 16th-century prodigy house was designed by Robert Smythson in the latest imported Renaissance style from the Low Countries. Classical columns, alcoves, Dutch gables and strapwork were copied from buildings like this and applied to houses of the lesser gentry.*

PLANS
Large houses

There was a dramatic change in the appearance of the houses of the nobility during the Tudor period from inward-looking, scattered buildings within a defensive courtyard to bold, symmetrical and lavish structures facing out to impress visitors. The more modest manor house of the Elizabethan Age showed less dramatic change, attempting to achieve a symmetrical façade, with a tall, roughly central porch standing the full height of, typically, two main storeys and a third attic floor, and with a large display of glass. With wings facing out at either end of larger examples this, in effect, created an E-shaped plan – although the Elizabethan gentry loved

Urban houses

The long, narrow plot of most urban houses meant there was only a short public face to the building. Height became the order of the day and these two, three and four storey houses could be made even more impressive by having the floors jettied out, one above the other. On most houses that were built lengthways down their plot, the most convenient way of covering it was with a series of pitched roofs running in the same direction, which left a gable end facing out onto the street. Some had more complex arrangements so that the pitch faced

FIG 3.3: *Tudor urban houses were usually built with the triangular gable end facing the road and jettied out over a couple of storeys. On wider plots a series of such gables could be used, or a conventional pitched roof as in the example here on the left. The front room on most of these properties would have been rented out as a shop.*

FIG 3.2: *Elevations of manor and larger country houses from the modest early Tudor façade at the top down to the later prodigy house at the bottom. Note that the bottom floor is roughly level with the ground and not raised up as would be common in later classically-inspired houses. These are new build houses; many others had elements of these added to existing structures.*

hidden meaning in their building (triangular plan structures implying the Trinity and devotion to the Catholic faith are a famous example), this was more a development of the medieval cross wings than any dedication to the queen.

Roof parallel to street

Gable end

Close studding

Jetty

Shop

Door leading to hall at rear.

the front, especially on wider plots, while others were small enough for this form to cover a whole row (although terraces like this were rare). Large houses and buildings with wider plots could emphasise this with continuous jetties along the whole façade, and long rows of glass windows. They might also feature oriels, sometimes with additional small windows flanking them either side.

FIG 3.4: *A cut away view of a gable-ended house, with the narrow front facing the road (top), and a house standing on a wider plot with a pitched roof and continuous jetty on its public façade.*

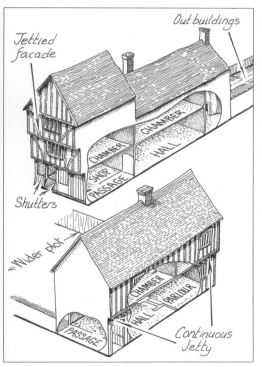

Rural houses

The houses of successful farmers were typically of two storeys, some with a third attic floor with large gabled dormer windows flush with the wall below. In some areas the large open hall or houseplace was still the main single room, but by the second half of the century most lowland houses had two principal ground floor rooms with chambers above.

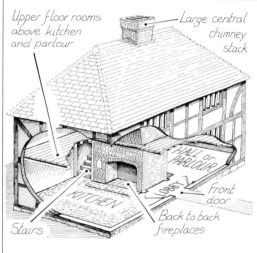

FIG 3.5: *A cutaway view of an axial plan farmhouse of a type that became popular across lowland England through the second half of the Tudor period.*

The position of the chimney was influential in the planning and its relationship with the original entrance can be indicative of the layout behind the façade. There were two general types of plan, the first of which had the door in line with a stout central chimney, a type that was popular in much of lowland England in the second half of the period. The second featured a cross passage from one side of the house to the other, with the fireplace either backing onto it or on a gable end – this was widely found in highland areas. Large T-shaped houses with or without a cross passage were built by yeoman farmers in parts of the West Midlands.

These rural houses with less restricted plots rarely survive today as originally planned. With rear extensions and side blocks added later they can appear much larger and the original arrangement can be tricky to trace. The smaller cottages of the labouring classes had just one or two rooms (only one would have been heated), some with a separate byre for livestock under the same roof.

STYLE OF FAÇADES

There were no distinct national styles in the Tudor period. Most houses were built under the influence of local craftsmen and vernacular designs passed down through generations, with new fashionable features slowly incorporated into their plans. The finest houses were more up-to-date but were of late medieval inspiration in the first half of the period, with forms and details from fortified and ecclesiastical buildings rather than the leading European designs.

FIG 3.7: MORETON CORBET, SHROPSHIRE: *This ruined Elizabethan building was the south range of an earlier castle and was begun by Robert Corbet in around 1578. He had travelled on the Continent, which was rare at this time, and the Renaissance features like the symmetrical façade and classical detailing reflect what he had seen on the ground and in books. The large gridwork windows, the horizontal string courses above each storey and the Dutch gables are features that would become more widely fashionable in the 17th century.*

FIG 3.6: *In the north of the country, tower houses derived from earlier more fortified pele towers were built by the lesser gentry and wealthy farmers, as in this example from the Peak District.*

FIG 3.8: WOOTTON LODGE, STAFFORDSHIRE: *A compact late Elizabethan house almost certainly designed by the master mason Robert Smythson (1536–1614). He was the nearest Tudor England got to producing an architect and apart from designing grand symmetrical classical houses was a genius in managing space. He was responsible for Wollaton Hall (1580–88), Hardwick Hall (1590–7) and the plans for Bolsover Castle (1612–27), which his son completed.*

On the Continent the rediscovery of the methods and style of design in Ancient Roman buildings, the Renaissance (rebirth), had begun to dramatically change the appearance of urban housing and country villas. These new classical designs based on ruins and old texts were reinterpreted by a new generation of architects who changed the way houses were planned and built. They applied symmetry across the front of the house and transferred the proportions of the different types of classical columns (the orders) into the horizontal divisions of the façade.

Although there are glimpses of this new approach to design in the reign of Henry VIII, the result of our separation from Rome was isolation from the main thrust of the Renaissance. Only in the second half of the 16th century do houses appear with symmetrical façades and some classical details. This development came, however, via the Low Countries (of Protestant persuasion like ourselves) from a limited number of men who had travelled there or the books available on the subject to the few craftsmen who could read them. They seem to have ignored the theory in the designs and just applied the classical details and general appearance of buildings to age-old plans rather than undertaking a radical redesigning of the structure.

Tudor brick and stone façades

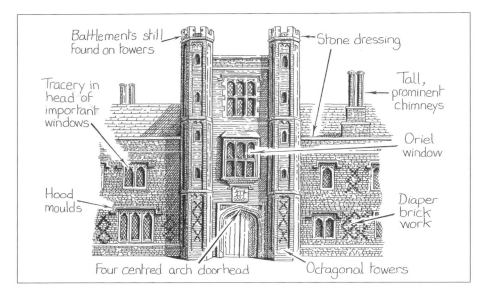

Battlements still found on towers

Tracery in head of important windows

Hood moulds

Stone dressing

Tall, prominent chimneys

Oriel window

Diaper brick work

Four centred arch doorhead

Octagonal towers

FIG 3.9: *A section of the façade of a typical early Tudor brick house with labels of some of its distinctive parts. Note that the arrangement of windows reflects the rooms behind it rather than their being positioned symmetrically.*

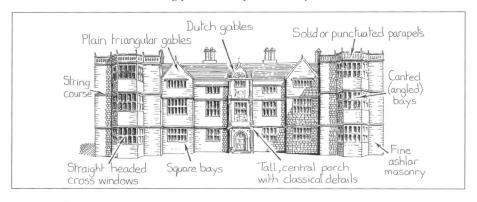

Dutch gables

Plain triangular gables

Solid or punctuated parapets

String course

Canted (angled) bays

Straight headed cross windows

Square bays

Tall, central porch with classical details

Fine ashlar masonry

FIG 3.10: *A typical large stone house built in the reign of Elizabeth I, with labels of some of the distinctive features from this period. Despite reflecting the influence of the Renaissance with the symmetrical façade, classical details and masses of glass, the building is still similar in form to earlier Tudor houses and the more modest manor houses of the lesser gentry.*

FIG 3.11: Towers and turrets were very popular, many with distinctive ogee-shaped caps as in this example.

FIG 3.12: *Tall chimneys and rows of pointed gables dominated the skyline of many Tudor houses. Chimneys came in all shapes and sizes, some plain, others highly decorated with a stepped feature at the top. Gables could be straight-sided or curved Dutch types (see fig 3.7), sometimes with finials on the top.*

FIG 3.13: *(below) An early Tudor stone window frame with a hood mould above (left) and a later example with a transom, diamond-shaped glass and a bold string course above (right).*

FIG 3.14: *(above) Diaper patterns formed with overheated grey bricks were very popular in the early Tudor period and then remained in use in more modest gentry houses even into the mid 17th century.*

FIG 3.15: *(right) Tall porches, with classical columns and decoration often crudely stacked upon each storey, are a characteristic feature of Elizabethan houses.*

FIG 3.16: *(below) A late Elizabethan doorway, with labels of some of the period features.*

FIG 3.17: *(below) A distinct form of decoration that was copied from houses in the Low Countries was strapwork. It was popular from about 1580–1620 and was derived from decorative book plates of leather straps.*

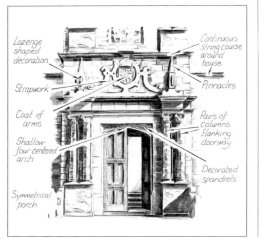

Lozenge shaped decoration

Strapwork

Coat of arms

Shallow four centered arch

Symmetrical porch

Continuous string course around house

Pinnacles

Pairs of columns flanking doorway

Decorated spandrels

Tudor timber frame style

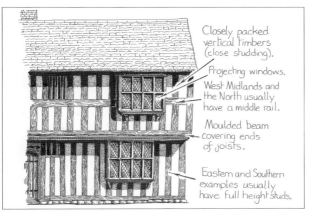

Closely packed vertical timbers (close studding).

Projecting windows.

West Midlands and the North usually have a middle rail.

Moulded beam covering ends of joists.

Eastern and Southern examples usually have full height studs.

FIG 3.18: *(left) A close-studded façade. This was the standard form of timber frame style in better quality housing in East Anglia from the 14th century, and was one that spread across much of the country, especially towns, during the Tudor period. It was a sign of wealth simply because it demonstrated that you could afford a lot of timber, although it was usually only used on the exposed front; a more simple form could be used on walls out of sight. In most parts the close studs ran the full height of each storey but in the West Midlands and some highland areas a horizontal middle rail ran halfway across. To stabilise the structure, braces were fitted on the inner face in the corners as on earlier styles, but out of sight.*

FIG 3.19: *(below) A square-panelled façade. An alternative style of timber framing was to divide up the box frame structure into smaller squares. These small square panels were popular in the Welsh border country and spread out to be used in many houses of the gentry and yeoman farmers from Sussex up to Cheshire during the 16th century. They could be further embellished with decorative inserts.*

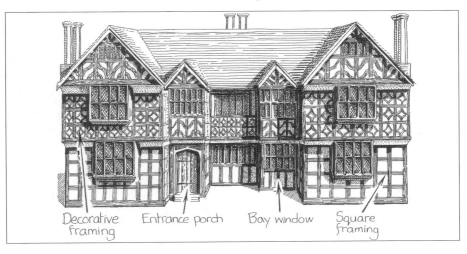

Decorative framing   Entrance porch   Bay window   Square framing

FIG 3.20: *(left) Examples of decorative framing, where patterns formed out of curved or profiled timber were inserted within square panelling (see fig 3.19). These decorative framed houses were built for wealthy clients and are common in Cheshire and Lancashire, with the finest displays on show at buildings like Little Moreton Hall (fig 2.1). The bargeboards along the edge of the gable could also be decorated, though this was common on all forms of framing.*

FIG 3.21: *Jetties are a distinctive feature of Tudor urban housing, but less so in the country. They were probably included more for status than any practical advantage gained from the increased space in the upper rooms. In the simplest form the joists on the lower ceiling are extended out by a few feet and the wall above rests on top of these with their ends exposed (below). On better quality houses the lower beam of this wall is joined onto the ends of the joists or a panel is applied to cover them up, with both being moulded or decorated (right).*

FIG 3.22: *Some large urban houses or rows of smaller properties were built with long continuous jetties across the whole façade. This example has a close-studded upper storey and exposed ends to the joists (the windows and doors are later additions).*

FIG 3.24: *Shallow projecting windows that were pegged to the frame were widely used. This example has a central transom and diamond shaped glass fitted in the lead cames.*

FIG 3.23: *In more prominent positions a jetty might continue down the side, in which case a diagonal joist would have to be fitted where the two faces met. This is called a dragon beam and although this example is plain many had the exposed end carved into a mystical beast or other decorative form.*

FIG 3.25: *It was fashionable in some high status buildings to have the glass panes formed into elaborate decorative schemes within each light, as in this example. Note the single opening casement in the lower central light.*

Dragon beam

CHAPTER 4

Tudor Interiors

ROOMS AND DETAILS

FIG 4.1: *A hall in a late Tudor farmhouse with a large inglenook fireplace, which heated the room and cooked the food. These were originally working spaces so if there were no specialised outbuildings then much of the process of preparing and storing meats and cheese would have taken place here as well as cooking and washing.*

The interior of a Tudor house would have struck someone used to today's standard of living as rather spartan, dark and pungent, although they might have been surprised at how colourful their surroundings were. The rooms passed through were linked directly to each other in most cases, with the largest houses containing a series of principal rooms leading to the private chamber of the owner, while in more modest houses a hall and parlour with sleeping accommodation above was typical. In most new houses there was a general move away from the communal living space of the medieval hall towards a more private, cleaner and better heated home, at the highest levels in the time of Henry VIII, and at yeoman class by the end of Elizabeth I's reign.

PRINCIPAL ROOMS

The communal hall, which had been the main element of large houses in the medieval period, began to lose importance, its role at the centre of the local estate lapsing now that tenants managed much of the land directly and required less contact with landowners. In the grandest Elizabethan houses it became no more than an impressive

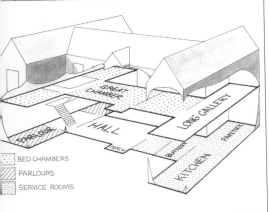

BED CHAMBERS
PARLOURS
SERVICE ROOMS

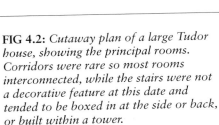

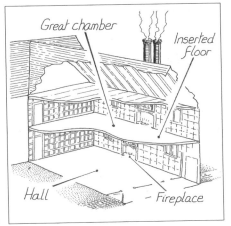

FIG 4.2: *Cutaway plan of a large Tudor house, showing the principal rooms. Corridors were rare so most rooms interconnected, while the stairs were not a decorative feature at this date and tended to be boxed in at the side or back, or built within a tower.*

FIG 4.3: *A cutaway view of a medieval hall (top) and the same room in the Tudor period after a floor has been inserted to create a great chamber above. Note the old central fire has been replaced in the Tudor house by separate fireplaces in both rooms.*

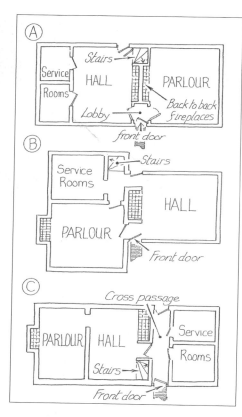

entrance space; in others it was retained for the use of lesser members of the household to take their meals. More attention was now given to a lavish great chamber where the owner could dine and entertain guests, with a withdrawing room where they could be received and a private bedchamber leading off this. Guests would move from one room to another during a visit – rather than eating, drinking and then collapsing asleep on the floor of a medieval hall!

There were also new rooms, such as the fashionable long galleries where they could take recreation and admire their surroundings or banqueting halls where sweets were eaten after the main meal. Both of these upper floor rooms celebrated the widespread use of glass with rows of windows giving grand views, the latter even in some cases being built on top of the roof!

In the houses of the lesser gentry the hall or houseplace was still the principal room, although a separate chamber for the family to take their meals was usually fitted on the floor above, with private bedchambers leading off this. The more modest farmhouse would typically have two main ground floor rooms: the hall, which was likely to be where much of the daily work was done and the parlour for relaxing and conversation (from the French verb *parler*, to speak). Urban houses contained the same rooms at the different social levels; however, with the restrictive long thin plot they were arranged in a row, usually with the hall towards the front on the ground floor, the private chambers above and service rooms behind (see fig 3.4 top).

FIG 4.4: *Three plans of houses built for successful farmers in the second half of the period. The axial plan (A) has a central chimney stack (see fig 3.5) with a small entrance lobby leading into a parlour on one side and a hall on the other, with stairs behind giving access to the bedchambers and loft above. The cross passage plan (C) popular in the highland region had access directly from front to back with the rooms leading off this and a fireplace either against the passage or an outer wall. The T-shaped plan (B) was often found in farmhouses in the North and West Midlands either with or without the cross passage.*

SERVICE ROOMS

Preparing the vast selection of courses for a Tudor feast required a range of service rooms and a large kitchen – as well as the healthy appetite of the gentrified family and their guests! The typical medieval arrangement, and one that could still be found in this period, was to have a buttery and pantry side by side at the far end of the hall away from where the owner sat, and behind or separate from this was the kitchen (these were often freestanding because of the fire risk). Tudor kitchens in the

FIG 4.6: *Long galleries were popular from the 1520s through into the mid 17th century. They gave owners and guests a view over gardens, and could be used as a secondary reception room or for exercise and private contemplation.*

FIG 4.5: *An elaborate, late Tudor, stone hall screen. Where a large hall was still built or in existing houses where it was retained, screens were fitted. These were barriers at the entrance end of the hall to keep draughts out when the doors were opened and typically had two openings – and a gallery above in larger houses for musicians to play on when entertaining guests. Timber versions were made from vertical posts with planks slotted in; more expensive types had square panelling, some with decorative mouldings.*

most up-to-date houses could now be found built into the main building, sometimes in a basement where the stone or brick walls and a vaulted ceiling could minimise the danger of fire.

In large houses there could also have been storage rooms, such as the buttery for drinks and pantry for foodstuffs, a bakehouse for making bread and a stillroom for the production of perfumes and medicines. A brewhouse was essential as water was not drunk, due to the health risk when not boiled, and milk was very rich (and most went to make cheese) so beer was the staple drink even at breakfast, varying in strength depending on the occasion.

In more modest houses there would not have been a separate kitchen; the cooking would have been done in one of the ground floor rooms. There would only have been basic cooking

FIG 4.7: *A kitchen from a large Tudor house. The large fireplace (A) with a spit (B) turned by hand or by an animal in a wheel would have dominated the room (wood was used in the fire as coal was expensive and reserved for private chambers). A bread oven (C) and a stove (D) in some kitchens would also have been used for cooking. There would have been little furniture other than the large central table (E).*

FIG 4.8: *The interior of a garderobe (left) and a view of one from the outside (right).*

These primitive toilets were generally fitted in tall extensions on the outside of large houses and had a dog-leg plan inside to help reduce odours, while the waste simply dropped down into the ditch or moat outside. There were also personal 'close stools' in or next to the bedchambers for the relief of the owner and his family, no more than elaborate lidded buckets! Despite these, one contemporary commentator noted that there was still 'too much pissing in chimneys'!

facilities as most meals were probably variations of a stew known as potage. Meat was a luxury enjoyed on a regular basis by the more successful farmer and above, rarely by those below. Fruit and vegetables were eaten, although limited to the periods when ripe, and fish was often restricted to the lord of the manor's table. Flat loaves of bread and home-made cheese seem to have been a main part of the staple diet for most working people. There were no washing-up facilities in the house so cooking utensils were just rinsed or wiped clean and any waste water poured down a hole in the ground outside called a sink (it was deep enough for the liquid to seep into the ground below the top soil in which crops were grown).

INTERIOR FEATURES

The rooms within a Tudor house were uncluttered by furniture; few had the money for it or the need to store possessions and those who did might still take the more valuable pieces – like the bed – with them as they moved from one of their properties to another. Tables were essential, however. The simple wooden trestles that had been universal in the medieval period were now being replaced in the finest houses by tables with large bulbous legs. Benches were still common, with chairs generally reserved for the owner (hence the modern day importance of the chairman) although they became more widespread towards the end of the period. Beds were four posters in the best houses; the curtains hung around the sides were used to keep out the draughts and to give a bit of privacy from the servants. There may have been a few cupboards and chests in the better houses – not too large, so they could be transported with other household items when the owner moved. There was little need for display, although in the finer houses good quality plate to impress diners was important (guests brought their own cutlery, consisting of just knives and spoons – hence the continuing custom of giving a silver spoon at christenings). Cupboards, which could have been used to store salt, spices or valuables, were built into the wall, under stairs or close to the fire to keep the damp away and often featured decorative carved doors.

Walls

In the important rooms of houses the walls were often covered by wooden panelling, especially in the hall of finer dwellings and the parlour of the farmhouse. Square shaped panels were the fashion in Tudor houses, with a rippling hung-fabric effect called linenfold being carved on the face of the wood (see fig 4.10). Later in the period smaller, plain panels became fashionable with decoration reserved for a frieze along the top edge, which could feature an arcaded pattern or strapwork. The frames into which the

panels slotted were pegged together with a moulded edge to the top and sides of each square and a flat chamfer at the bottom to make it easier to dust (look for these to identify original work as they were often missed off replicas or are in the wrong position if the panelling has been moved).

The dark stained wood and bright white walls we see today are a later fashion – in most Tudor houses the important rooms would have been as colourful as the exterior surfaces could be. Wooden panelling was usually painted and the plain walls had decorative patterns brushed on, many of which have been uncovered when renovating old houses. Pictures

FIG 4.9: *A close up of wooden panelling, showing how the moulding runs around the top and sides of each square but the bottom is a flush chamfer to make cleaning easier. At this date skirting boards were not fitted at the bottom so where they are found it is likely to be a later addition.*

FIG 4.10: *Linenfold wall panelling, which was popular in the first half of the Tudor period.*

often covered with rushes or cheaper coverings, which could be scented and then replaced every month or so when they had become too dirty.

The ceiling was usually the underside of the floorboards above and the ceiling beams and joists that supported them. The main bridging beam was the largest piece of timber in the house and was usually chamfered on its underside. Better examples might have mouldings, a decorative boss fitted and even the arrangement of the joists to form a pattern. These beams were also likely to have been colourfully painted in many important rooms. In the finest later Tudor houses a ceiling was sometimes fitted to cover these

were rarely hung upon the walls, and it was not until later in the period that family portraits for the wealthy became fashionable. Many of the finest Tudor houses also had tapestries hung over the walls.

Floors and ceilings

The ground floor of most houses would have been no more than beaten earth with a mixture applied to harden it. In better houses stone flags were laid, and tiles could have been used in the finest. Floorboards were fitted in important rooms like the parlour and on top of the joists for upper chambers. They were generally wide planks at this date, up to a foot across and butted into each other, although there was a gradual move by the end of the period towards thinner and more regular sized ones. Ground floors even in the finest houses were

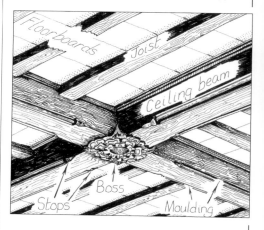

FIG 4.11: *A ceiling from a Tudor house with labels of its parts and decoration. An example like this, with carefully arranged joists, mouldings and a boss, would have been fitted in a principal room of a wealthy householder. In some cases ceiling boards would be fitted between or on top of the joists to create a flat surface, which could then be painted with decorative patterns.*

beams and a plaster pattern applied to it. A few early examples with shallow designs can be found but by the end of the 16th century they start to become deep set with geometric shaped panels, interweaving guilloche or strapwork designs.

FIG 4.12: *A plastered ceiling from an Elizabethan house with distinctive shallow geometric mouldings (late 16th and early 17th-century examples had much deeper profiles).*

Stairs

As houses of two or three storeys became common so a set of stairs was required. They had been fitted in larger medieval houses, but a ladder had sufficed in others if there was an upper floor. In Tudor houses they tended to be compact structures enclosed by walls and not made into a feature. They could be either a winder stair, as was built into axial plan houses beside the fireplace, or a newel stair, which was similar but the treads and risers were fixed into a vertical newel post. Larger houses might have the stairs built into turrets and towers, with windows illuminating the ascent,

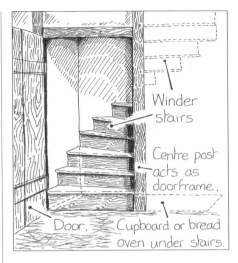

FIG 4.13: *Drawings of a winder stair (top) as found tucked into the corners of axial plan houses and a closed well stair (bottom) found in larger ones. Many had doors fitted across the bottom and top, larger ones that did not may have had a dog-gate to keep the animals downstairs at night.*

sometimes with separate ones for the owner and the servants. These houses usually had a central well, which would make the stairs seem more impressive, but at this date most of these were originally walled in, sometimes with cupboards fitted within to make use of the space. Decorative balusters and handrails occasionally appeared in the late 16th century, but these would be a key feature of later Jacobean houses.

Fireplaces

The fireplace became the must have new feature of Tudor houses. The finest medieval houses and castles could be found with them but most had central hearths in the hall, and it was only when these had a room fitted above that the fire had to move up against a wall and be set within a recessed opening (these were also more effective at removing the more offensive fumes from coal, which was now more widely available). Where fitted centrally, they often had back-to-back fireplaces; when built onto an external wall the fireplace opening projected out and a garderobe was sometimes fitted next to it for convenience of building and to keep the small toilet warm. Most houses, though, did not have heating upstairs and, in larger houses where fireplaces were fitted in bed chambers, they were rarely lit. Alternatives to the fireplace that could still be found in this period were a hood fitted to the wall with the hearth below and not recessed or a smoke bay in which one end of the hall (usually the screen passage) was enclosed to trap the fumes.

The fireplace surround was built flush with the wall, generally with no mantelpiece. A stone four-centred arch (as with doors) was a popular

FIG 4.14: *A stone fireplace surround typically with a very shallow four centred arch on its inner profile (top) and a brick chimney with a more defined arch formed from individual bricks (bottom). Note the herringbone pattern on the fireback of the latter example, a feature often found on late medieval and Tudor fireplaces.*

profile; the spandrels were either plain, sunken or filled with a pattern, heraldic earlier and foliage designs later. The moulding around the edge characteristically stopped only a short way down the sides on Elizabethan examples. Brick fireplaces have similar shapes but are generally just plain flat arches, although some originally may have been plastered to resemble stone. Many had brick or stone jambs but with a large timber lintel across the top (see fig 4.1), sometimes beautifully carved.

The fireplace itself was often a large inglenook, which gave space for benches and shelves to keep food warm. It was also common for bread ovens to be built to one side. The fire was supported off the ground by fire-dogs or held in a basket in the case of coal. Towards the end of the period cast iron firebacks, which helped protect the back of the fireplace and reflect heat into the room, were introduced. The most distinctive feature of later Tudor fireplaces in the more important room is an overmantel. These are decorative wooden or plaster panels directly above the opening and often incorporating its surround, with arches or geometric shapes being popular.

FIG 4.15: *Late 16th and early 17th-century fireplaces in large houses often featured a decorated overmantel above the fireplace surround.*

CHAPTER 5

Tudor Gardens

••◦◦◦••

OUTBUILDINGS AND GATEHOUSES

FIG 5.1: *A view from a large Tudor house, overlooking the rear space. A knot garden comprising geometric spaces formed by low hedges is flanked on either side by a raised walkway (left) and an arbour (right). In the rear left corner is a pavilion used as a banqueting room and on the right is a mount with a spiral walkway leading up to a timber building from which the garden can be better appreciated. At the centre rear is a maze – these were featured in some large gardens, though usually with low hedges at this date.*

The space directly surrounding the house had previously been of little aesthetic value and was only beginning to be appreciated as such in the finer Tudor home. The area around the house was a working space – either a courtyard with scattered buildings looking in upon it or a plot of land to grow produce and keep livestock. Gardens were not unknown before; a small enclosed space for growing herbs and scented flowers was common alongside larger medieval houses and abbeys

FIG 5.2: *Examples of knot gardens recreated at Newstead Abbey (top) and Little Moreton Hall (bottom).*

the larger-scale landscaping of later grand houses.

Most used the Renaissance-inspired symmetrical plan, bordered by a tall boundary and divided within into squares and geometric shapes by low hedges or parterres to form knot gardens. There might be lawn, gravel, coloured sands, broken bricks, or a limited range of flowers within these. The path that bordered them often had an arbour over part of it, with climbing plants like roses creating a sweet-scented tunnel to walk through, not a bad idea at a time of poor drainage. The fashion for mazes at the highest level of design meant that smaller ones were built in more modest gardens. Somewhere around the edge or in a corner, a raised area or mound was built, usually with a structure on top from which the garden and surrounding countryside could be admired.

FIG 5.3: *Raised mounts were an important feature in Tudor gardens and could be huge, carefully constructed viewpoints. A spiral path or steps led up to some form of cover on top, probably a simple lightweight structure as here but in some cases enclosed buildings were erected.*

and a walled garden used for quiet contemplation was often squeezed in on many sites. The idea of planning large areas front and back became important as soon as the design of the large house changed from an inward looking structure to an outward display of wealth and ambition. Gardens became a fashionable addition, although at this date they were still small in comparison with

FIG 5.4: *Examples of garden buildings dating from the late 16th (top) and early 17th century (bottom) – the windows on the top example are later. They probably served as banqueting and summerhouses and were typically built alongside the wall surrounding the garden.*

GARDEN BUILDINGS

One of the most characteristic features to be found in Tudor gardens is a banqueting house. These could be built as pavilions in the corners of the outer garden wall or as freestanding structures ranging from single rooms to almost small houses. They were used in the same way as the banqueting rooms built within the house, a place to retire to after the main meal where sweets could be eaten, and some also as summerhouses from which to admire the surroundings.

GATEHOUSES

Another key building was the gatehouse. This was a vital defensive feature in medieval fortified homes and provided luxury accommodation for an important member of the

FIG 5.5: *An early Tudor gatehouse at Lambeth Palace, London. Unlike medieval defensive structures the walls here are perforated with windows.*

FIG 5.6: *Examples of gatehouses dating from the late 16th and early 17th centuries at Burton Agnes Hall, Yorkshire (left), Long Melford Hall, Suffolk (bottom right) and Stokesay Castle, Shropshire (bottom left). As demonstrated by the decorative features and numerous windows they had little to do with defence and more to do with impressing guests.*

household. Although its defensive qualities were of little importance in the more settled Tudor times the tall and imposing gatehouse was still built across the entrance to the drive or courtyard. Most that can be seen today are in stone or brick, with characteristic towers and turrets in the corners, and a four-centred arched opening below. Timber framed examples were probably numerous but only a few examples have survived.

CHAPTER 6

Tudor Houses

AFTER 1603

Tudor houses today rarely survive in their original form, four centuries of increased demands upon accommodation and changing fashions have partially or radically altered them. Farmhouses were often extended by either adding a bay or two at the ends or single storey rooms at the back; others were rebuilt, with successful farmers erecting stout brick and stone houses as their old timber framed homes now looked out of date. When villages were reorganised in the more widespread enclosures of the 18th and 19th century, new farmhouses were built out in the fields, with the now unfashionable Tudor structures back in the village used by farm labourers and sometimes sub-divided into smaller cottages.

Larger Tudor houses quickly went out of date in a society that had little time or appreciation for old buildings. By the second half of the 17th century classical architecture dominated the finest houses and the exuberant Baroque and later refined Palladian style, with their more correct use of proportions, large sash windows and a wider availability of brick and stone, meant that even some of the classically-inspired houses of the Elizabethan period looked clumsy and unfashionable. Many country houses were refaced to mask their Tudor core, with new extensions further disguising their origins. More modest manor houses might not go so far but new sash windows and some classical details like a porch could easily be added. Other

FIG 6.1: *This house in Buckinghamshire, known as Tudor Cottage, is believed to have been part of a larger 16th-century timber framed farmhouse. It is likely that when the area was enclosed it was divided into two farm labourers' cottages, the left-hand one of which was replaced by a new brick house in the 1800s. Around this time the remaining section had a lower pitch slate roof fitted, bricks replaced its wattle and daub infills and the black and white paint scheme was applied, creating the building that still stands today.*

FIG 6.2: LYME PARK, CHESHIRE:
This Elizabethan country house (the porch on the north range is shown in fig 3.15) was radically altered in the 1720s with a new classical south range, illustrated above, and other changes that disguise the earlier, smaller 16th century house. Nearby Chatsworth, once one of the homes of Bess of Hardwick, was similarly remodelled in the late 17th century to create the classical country house we see today.

landowners, though, abandoned their earlier houses, especially those that were timber framed, and simply built a new Georgian or Victorian house, with the Tudor house often becoming a farmhouse.

In towns and cities timber framed Tudor houses not only looked unfashionable but also were a fire risk. After the Great Fire of London in 1666 many local authorities began applying the same regulations as the capital, and those dwellings that had not burnt down were gradually replaced anyway by more fire-resistant brick and stone structures. On main roads where inns,

FIG 6.3: *This old, timber framed inn on the busy London to Oxford coach route was refaced in the 18th century to appear more up-to-date (top). The old timber frame, though, can be seen at the rear (bottom). You can usually tell where this has been done as the windows on the front are not neatly lined up as on a new classical house or they show signs of sagging with the old timber frame beneath. It was also common for just the front to be refaced so a quick walk down the side or at the back, as in the second view from behind this inn, reveals its true origins.*

houses that a new generation of young architects studied in the countryside inspired them to create new forms of house with asymmetrical façades, mixes of timber framing, stone and brick and casement rather than sash windows. Many of these personalities went on to become part of the Arts and Crafts movement and help form the

FIG 6.4: CAPESTHORNE, CHESHIRE: *built in the 1830s in the style of the late 16th and early 17th centuries, this was an early example of the revivalist architecture that would come to dominate the Victorian period.*

Tall chimneys.

Long, low slung roofs

Prominent gable to the front.

Elongated, low dormers.

Staggered sides of window frames.

Mullioned windows.

Mix of material (Stone and Timber)

FIG 6.5: *An urban house designed in the 1890s and featuring many Tudor details, such as the timber framing and mullion windows. Many of these late Victorian houses are so close to the original Tudor buildings that they can at first glance be hard to differentiate. Most, however, tend to have mock timber cladding on the upper storey only, with the lower in brick or stone, whereas originals would have had a complete timber frame. The wood is also usually straight and unworn, but you would expect the unseasoned oak used in a genuine Tudor house to be bowed, split and show signs of age. Victorian bricks will be sharp edged and regular, unlike the thinner, uneven and richly textured types used in the 16th century.*

hostelries and shops had to attract coach traffic by appearing up-to-date, owners who could not afford to rebuild their old timber framed buildings had them faced over with an up-to-date classical façade. In other areas a similar effect was achieved by nailing weatherboarding to the outside or hanging mathematical tiles to simulate brickwork or at least replacing the old infill with new brick panels.

The revivalist movements of the later Victorian period began to reverse this decline in fortune. A growing appreciation for old buildings and their picturesque setting created an affection for many Tudor houses. The glories of the Elizabethan Age were relived as late 16th-century-style houses were created in the decades after the Napoleonic Wars.

By the 1860s the old farm and manor

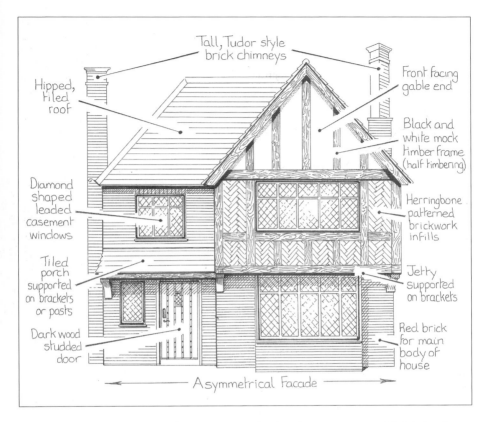

Tall, Tudor style brick chimneys

Hipped, tiled roof

Diamond shaped leaded casement windows

Tiled porch supported on brackets or posts

Dark wood studded door

Front facing gable end

Black and white mock timber frame (half timbering)

Herringbone patterned brickwork infills

Jetty supported on brackets

Red brick for main body of house

← Asymmetrical Facade →

FIG 6.6: *A Tudor-style house from a 1920s suburban housing estate with labels of some of its fashionable features.*

National Trust and the Society for the Preservation of Ancient Buildings, who in turn played their part in creating the 20th-century ethos of protecting and restoring our heritage.

In the Edwardian period this revival of Tudor style worked its way down to the mass housing market, with the latest large terrace houses featuring mock timber gables and tiled roofs. By the 1920s this had spread to become a dominant style for the new semi-

detached houses that were springing up in suburban areas around major towns and cities. Again the Tudor style used consisted of details applied to a modern structure, but it did emphasise the nation's growing affection for this period and its need to cloak itself in the past to seek protection from the future. Elements of these houses can still be found in the timber gables and leaded windows on housing estates today.

GLOSSARY

ASHLAR: Smooth, squared stone masonry with fine joints.

AXIAL: A feature located or a plan laid out along the axis of a house.

BALUSTER: Plain or decorated post supporting the stair rail.

BALUSTRADE: A row of decorated uprights (balusters) with a rail along the top.

BARGEBOARDS: External vertical boards that protected the ends of the sloping roof on a gable and were often decorated.

BAY: A vertical division of a house between trusses. Usually reflected on the façade by a column of windows.

BAY WINDOW: A window projecting from the façade of a house up a single or number of storeys and usually resting on the ground.

BONDING: The way bricks are laid in a wall, with the different patterns formed by alternative arrangements of headers (the short ends) and stretchers (the long side).

BOW WINDOW: A vertical projection (bay) of semi-circular or segmental plan.

CAMES: Strips of lead which hold the individual panes of glass in a leaded window.

CAPITAL: The decorated top of a classical column.

CASEMENT: A window that is hinged along the side.

CHAMFER: A straight diagonal cut along a corner of an opening to remove the sharp edge.

CHIMNEYPIECE: An internal fireplace surround.

CORNICE: The top section of the entablature, which in this context refers to the moulding that runs around the top of an external or internal wall.

COVING: A large concave moulding which covers the joint between the top of a wall and ceiling.

CRUCK: A type of timber framed building in which the roof structure is carried upon two matching beams positioned to form an upside-down 'V', with the wall bracketed off this. Popular in the medieval period it was becoming rare by the 16th century and was primarily used in smaller houses in the west and north of England.

DRAGON BEAM: A diagonal joist underneath jetties which meet at a corner of a house.

DORMER: An upright window set in the angle of the roof and casting light into the attic rooms.

EAVES: The section of the roof timbers under the tiles or slates where they either meet the wall (and a parapet continues above) or project over it (usually protected by a fascia board, which supports the guttering).

ENTABLATURE: The horizontal lintel supported by columns in a classical temple.

FAÇADE: The main vertical face of the house.

FENESTRATION: The arrangement of windows in the facade of a house.

FINIAL: An ornamental piece on top of a railing or the end of the roof ridge.

FLUTING: The vertical concave grooves running up a column or pilaster.

FOUR-CENTRED ARCH: A popular, nearly flat, arch which comprises two short radii where it springs from the sides of the opening and two large radii meeting at a point in the centre.

FRIEZE: The middle section of the entablature, in this context referring to the section of the wall between the picture rail and cornice.

GABLE: The pointed upper section of wall at the end of a pitched roof.

GLAZING BARS: The internal divisions of a window, which support the panes.

GUILLOCHE: A decorative pattern made from two twisted bands forming circles between.

HALF TIMBERING: A form of building construction with timber sections strengthened by braces.

HEARTH: The stone or brick base of a fireplace.

JAMBS: The sides of an opening for a door or window.

JOISTS: Horizontal beams that support the floorboards and are exposed in many Tudor houses in the room below.

KEYSTONE: The top stone in an arch, often projected as a feature.

LINTEL: A flat beam that is fitted above a door or window to take the load of the wall above.

MOULDING: A decorative strip of wood, stone or plaster.

MULLION: A vertical member dividing a window.

NEWEL: The principal vertical post in a set of stairs.

ORIEL: A large projecting window supported from the wall on an upper storey.

PARAPET: The top section of wall which continues above the sloping end of the roof.

PARGETING: A raised pattern formed from plaster on an external wall (popular originally in the East of England).

PARTERRE: The square sections of a Tudor garden formed from low hedges filled with shrubs and gravel to form patterns within.

PEDIMENT: A low pitched triangular feature supported by columns or pilasters above a classically styled door or window in this context.

PILASTER: A flat classical column fixed to a wall or fireplace and projecting slightly from it.

PINTLE: The vertical pin held on a bracket fitted in the jamb of a doorway onto which the hook at the end of a strap hinge was fitted.

PITCH: The angle by which a roof slopes. A plain sloping roof of two sides is called a pitched roof.

PLINTH: The projecting base around a building.

PRODIGY HOUSE: A modern term coined to describe the large, extravagant houses built by courtiers usually trying to gain favour with Queen Elizabeth I.

PURLIN: A horizontal timber beam that runs along the pitch of a roof.

QUARREL: A single pane of glass, in the case of Tudor houses usually diamond-shaped, which is fitted in lead cames to form a leaded window.

QUOINS: The corner stones at the junction of walls. Often raised above the surface, made from contrasting materials or finished differently from the rest of the wall for decorative effect.

RAFTERS: Inclined beams running from the top of the wall up to the apex, which support the roof covering on top of them. Principal rafters form the upper part of most trusses.

RENDER: A protective covering for a wall.

REVEAL: The sides (jambs) of a recessed window or door opening.

SASH WINDOW: A window of two separate sashes which slide vertically (or horizontally on smaller Yorkshire Sash windows).

SKIRTING: The protective strip of wood at the base of a wall.

SPANDREL: The triangular-shaped area above an arch which is usually recessed or filled with decoration, especially above important doorways.

STRAPWORK: Flat bands forming decorative patterns on stone buildings from the 1580s to the 1620s.

STRING COURSE: A horizontal band running across a façade and usually projecting.

TRACERY: The ribs that divide the top of a stone window and are formed into patterns.

TRANSOM: The horizontal bar in a window.

TRUSS: A triangular frame of timber beams supporting the roof.

VAULT: An arched structure of brick or stone used to cover a room or commonly to form the ceiling of basement or cellars.

VERNACULAR: Buildings made from local materials in styles and methods of construction passed down within a distinct area, as opposed to architect designed structures made from mass-produced materials.

VOUSSOIR: The wedged shaped stones or bricks that make up an arch.

WAINSCOT: Timber lining of internal walls or panelling.

BIBLIOGRAPHY

There is a wealth of books and internet sites covering all aspects of Tudor and Elizabethan houses; the few listed here are some of the publications that I have found useful:

The Buildings of England series by Sir Nikolaus Pevsner and others. A comprehensive architectural guide to each county, the updated versions, where available, giving an impressively detailed survey for most towns and villages. Published originally by Penguin but now by Yale University Press.

Malcolm Airs *The Tudor and Jacobean Country House: A Building History* 1995
John Anthony *Discovering Period Gardens* 1997
R.W. Brunskill *Brick Building in Britain* 1997
Richard Harris *Discovering Timber Framed Buildings* 1979
David Iredale and John Barrett *Discovering Your Old House* 1991
Norah Lofts *Domestic Life in England* 1976
Nigel Nicolson *The National Trust Book of Great Houses of Britain* 1978
Richard Reid *The Shell Book of Cottages* 1977
Alison Sim *Food and Feast in Tudor England* 1997

Also published by Countryside Books (available at www.countrysidebooks.co.uk):

Bill Breckon and Jeffrey Parker *Tracing the History of Houses* 2000
Linda Hall *Period House Fixtures and Fittings* 2005
Trevor Yorke *The Country House Explained* 2003, *The Victorian House Explained* 2005, *The Edwardian House Explained* 2006, *The 1930s House Explained* 2006, *Georgian and Regency Houses Explained* 2007, *British Architectural Styles* 2008

Apart from the wide range of houses to visit maintained by the National Trust, English Heritage, local authorities and private owners there are two museums of note that I would recommend visiting to see timber framed buildings in their original form:

AVONCROFT MUSEUM OF HISTORIC BUILDINGS, Stoke Heath, Bromsgrove, Worcestershire, B60 4JR; 01527 831363/ 831886; www.avoncroft.org.uk

WEALD AND DOWNLAND OPEN AIR MUSEUM, Town Lane, Singleton, West Sussex, PO18 OEU; 01243 811363; www.wealddown.co.uk
An outstanding collection of houses from all periods, especially rural buildings, and including displays on how bricks were made in this period.

Index

Also in the Living History Series

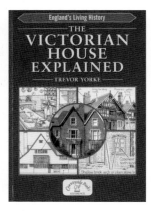

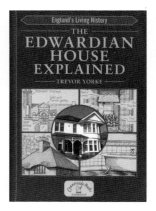

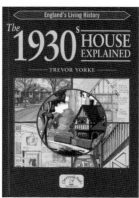

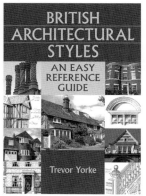

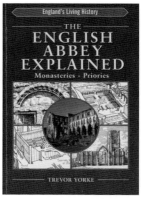

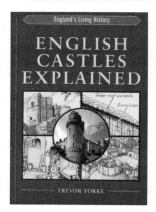

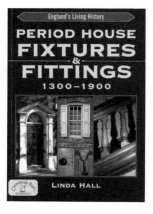

To view our complete range of books, please visit us at
www.countrysidebooks.co.uk